# PAUL MEALOR

*Selections from*

# *A Tender Light*

*for SATB chorus*

*A Tender Light is dedicated, with gracious permission,*

*to Their Royal Highnesses*

*The Duke and Duchess of Cambridge*

Published by:
**Novello Publishing Limited**
14-15 Berners Street, London W1T 3LJ, UK.

Exclusive Distributors:
**Music Sales Limited**
Distribution Centre, Newmarket Road,
Bury St. Edmunds, Suffolk IP33 3YB, UK.
**Music Sales Pty Limited**
20 Resolution Drive, Caringbah, NSW 2229, Australia.

Order No. NOV200926
ISBN 978-1-78038-442-9


Edited by Tom Farncombe.
Music processed by Paul Ewers Music Design.
With thanks to Hywel Davies and John Blood.
Photos page 3 by Tyson Benton and
page 80 by Jillian Bain Christie.

Printed in the EU.

***Novello Publishing Limited***
PART OF THE MUSIC SALES GROUP
London / New York / Paris / Sydney / Copenhagen / Berlin / Madrid / Hong Kong / Tokyo

ppp
ppp
ppp

# PAUL MEALOR

(b. 1975)

Paul Mealor's music is performed by choirs and singers around the world. He has been described by the *New York Times* as 'one of the most important composers to have emerged in Welsh choral music since William Mathias'. His music, infused with his deep Christian beliefs, is said to have 'serene beauty and architectural assuredness.' His motet *Ubi caritas*, written for the Royal Wedding of TRH The Duke and Duchess of Cambridge, reached No.1 in the UK Classical Singles Chart and has already entered the standard repertoire of many choirs. Mealor is Professor of Composition at the University of Aberdeen and divides his time between homes in the North of Scotland and North Wales – the landscapes of both having a great effect on his work.

Perfformir cerddoriaeth Paul Mealor gan gorau a chantorion o gwmpas y byd. Fe'i disgrifiwyd gan y *New York Times* fel 'un o'r cyfansoddwyr pwysicaf i ddod allan o gerddoriaeth corawl Gymreig ers William Mathias'. Dywedir bod ei gerddoriaeth, a lenwir gan ei gredoau Cristnogol, â 'phrydferthwch tawel a sicrwydd pensaernïol.' Cyrhaeddodd ei anthem *Ubi caritas*, a gyfansoddwyd ar gyfer Priodas Frenhinol EHB Dug a Duges Caergrawnt, rif 1 yn Siart Senglau Clasurol y DU ac erbyn hyn mae wedi dod yn rhan o stoc safonol llawer o gorau. Mae Mealor yn Athro Cyfansoddi ym Mhrifysgol Aberdeen ac mae'n rhannu ei amser rhwng cartrefi yng Ngogledd Yr Alban a Gogledd Cymru – mae tirweddau'r ddwy wedi cael effaith fawr ar ei waith.

**NOTES ON THE MUSIC BY PAUL MEALOR**
**NODIADAU AR Y GERDDORIAETH GAN PAUL MEALOR**

# Now Sleeps the Crimson Petal

(2010)
Four Madrigals on Rose Texts

## No. I:
## Now sleeps the crimson petal

Now sleeps the crimson petal, now the white;
Nor waves the cypress in the palace walk;
Nor winks the gold fin in the porphyry font:
The firefly wakens: waken thou with me.

Now droops the milkwhite peacock like a ghost,
And like a ghost she glimmers on to me.
Now lies the Earth all Danae to the stars,
And all thy heart lies open unto me.

Now folds the lily all her sweetness up,
And slips into the bosom of the lake:
So fold thyself, my dearest, thou, and slip
Into my bosom and be lost in me.
*Alfred, Lord Tennyson*

## No. II:
## Lady, when I behold the roses sprouting

Lady, when I behold the roses sprouting,
Which clad in damask mantles deck the arbours,
And then behold your lips where sweet love harbours,
My eyes present me with a double doubting;
For, viewing both alike, hardly my mind supposes
Whether the roses be your lips or your lips the roses.
*Anon.*

## No. III:
## Upon a bank with roses

Upon a bank with roses set about
Where pretty turtles joining bill to bill,
And gentle springs steal softly murmuring out,
Washing the foot of pleasures sacred hill.
There little Love sore wounded lies.
His bow and arrows broken,
Bedewed with tears from Venus' eyes.
O grievous to be spoken.
*John Ward*

## No. IV:
## A Spotless Rose

A Spotless Rose is growing,
Sprung from a tender root,
Of ancient seers' foreshowing,
Of Jesse promised fruit;
Its fairest bud unfolds to light
Amid the cold, cold winter,
And in the dark midnight.
The Rose which I am singing,
Where of Isaiah said,
Is from its sweet root springing
In Mary, purest Maid;
Through God's great love and might
The Blessed Babe she bare us
In a cold, cold winter's night. Amen
*Anon.*

The four texts for this short choral cycle are all connected by roses – either directly, or as a metaphor for love. *Now sleeps the crimson petal*, is an erotic, sensual poem that compares human beauty to that of the rose and lily – the closing of the lily representing the union of two lovers. *Lady, when I behold the roses sprouting* compares a woman's red lips to that of the deep, red rose. I allow the woman herself a voice when, on the repeat of the poem, a wordless soprano offers a short lament. *Upon a Bank* presents an idyllic scene of a trickling brook with roses set around it and small turtledoves kissing; however, 'love' is wounded and, even surrounded by this beautiful setting, he cannot be appeased. The final movement, *A Spotless Rose*, is the emotional heart of the cycle, and recalls the music of the previous movements. The 'Spotless Rose' of the poem is the baby Jesus and this poem is a celebration of him and the Blessed Virgin. It is has often been set as a Christmas carol. The first bars of my setting represent in music the petals of a rose opening in all directions, before reaching a climax at the words, 'fairest bud unfolds to light'.

Cysylltir y pedwar testun ar gyfer y cylch corawl byr hwn gan rosynnau – naill ai'n uniongyrchol, neu fel trosiad am gariad. Mae *Nawr cwsg y petal rhuddgoch* yn gerdd erotig, nwydus sy'n cymharu prydferthwch dynol â phrydferthwch y rhosyn a'r lili – mae'r lili'n cau'n cynrychioli uniad dau gariad. Mae *Foneddiges, pan wyf yn gweld y rhosynnau'n egino'n* cymharu gwefusau coch menyw â gwefusau'r rhosyn coch, dwfn. Rwyf yn caniatáu llais i'r fenyw ei hunan pan yw soprano ddi-air yn cynnig galarnad fer wrth i'r gerdd ailadrodd. Mae *Ar Lan* yn cynrychioli golygfa odidog â nant ddiferol arhosynnau wedi'u gosod o'i chwmpas a thurturod bach yn cusanu; fodd bynnag, mae 'cariad' wedi'i glwyfo ac, hyd yn oed ei fod wedi'i gwmpasu gan y gosodiad prydferth hwn, ni ellir ei dawelu. Y symudiad terfynol, *Rhosyn Di-staen*, yw calon emosiynol y cylch, ac mae'n ad-alw cerddoriaeth y symudiadau blaenorol. 'Rhosyn Di-staen' y gerdd yw'r baban Iesu ac mae'r gerdd hon yn ddathliad ohono ac o Fair Forwyn. Yn aml mae wedi'i threfnu fel carol Nadolig. Mae bariau cyntaf fy nhrefniant yn cynrychioli mewn cerddoriaeth betalau'r rhosyn sy'n agor ymhob cyfeiriad, cyn cyrraedd uchafbwynt â'r geiriau, 'eginyn tecach yn agor i'r goleuni'.

# She walks in beauty
(2010)

She walks in beauty, like the night
Of cloudless climes and starry skies;
And all that's best of dark and bright
Meet in her aspect and her eyes:
Thus mellowed to that tender light
Which heaven to gaudy day denies.

One shade the more, one ray the less,
Had half impaired the nameless grace
Which waves in every raven tress,
Or softly lightens o'er her face;
Where thoughts serenely sweet express
How pure, how dear their dwelling place.

And on that cheek, and o'er that brow,
So soft, so calm, yet eloquent,
The smiles that win, the tints that glow,
But tell of days in goodness spent,
A mind at peace with all below,
A heart whose love is innocent!
*Lord Byron*

I fell in love with this poem when I was a schoolboy and knew that one day I would set it! Lord Byron combines opposites in perfect proportions to compare a woman with a starry night. She brings together these opposites in her beauty and creates a 'tender light.' My eight-part setting tries to capture Byron's amazement at such beauty. Through a constantly changing aural focus of C and G major with added major and minor seconds it attempts to convey the 'opposites' of light and darkness present in this woman's beauty.

Syrthiais mewn cariad â'r gerdd hon pan oeddwn yn fachgen ysgol a gwyddwn y byddwn yn ei threfnu un diwrnod! Mae'r Arglwydd Byron yn cyfuno pethau cyferbyniol mewn cyfrannau perffaith er mwyn cymharu menyw â nos serennog. Mae hi'n cyfuno'r pethau cyferbyniol hyn yn ei phrydferthwch gan greu 'goleuni tyner'. Mae fy nhrefniant o wyth rhan yn ceisio cipio rhyfeddod Byron ar weld y fath brydferthwch. Trwy newid ffocws clywedol o C mwyaf a G mwyaf yn gyson, ag eiliadau mwyaf a lleiaf ychwanegol mae'n ceisio cyfleu'r 'pethau cyferbyniol' o oleuni a thywyllwch sy'n bresennol ym mhrydferthwch y fenyw hon.

# O vos omnes
(2011)

O vos omnes qui transitis per viam:
attendite et videte si est dolor sicut dolor meus.

O vos omnes qui transitis per viam, attendite et
videte: Si est dolor similis sicut dolor meus.

Attendite, universi populi, et videte dolorem meum.
Si est dolor similis sicut dolor meus.

Hinei ma tov u-ma n aim, shevet achim gam yachad

*O all ye that pass by the way, attend and*
*see if there be any sorrow like to my sorrow.*

*O all ye that pass by the way, attend and see:*
*If there be any sorrow like to my sorrow.*

*Attend, all ye people, and see my sorrow:*
*If there be any sorrow like to my sorrow.*

*Behold how good, and how pleasant it is,*
*for brothers to dwell together in unity.*

The Book of Lamentations, from which this text is drawn, is the darkest chapter in all Scripture. The book paints a picture of The Holy City, Jerusalem, in sorrow and desolation: 'She weeps bitterly in the night; And her tears are on her cheeks'. There are, however, glimmers of hope; that by looking upon this sorrow, by paying attention ('*attendite*' in Latin is sung five times in this piece, representing the five times it appears in the Book of Lamentations) we may be set free from pain. I have chosen to set the text in both Latin and English with the addition of a line from Psalm 133 in Hebrew near the end. I added this to present a glimmer of hope for the Holy Lands: 'Behold how good, and how pleasant it is, for brothers to dwell together in unity.'

Llyfr Galarnadau, y tynnwyd y testun hwn ohono, yw'r bennod dywyllaf yn yr holl Ysgrythur. Mae'r llyfr yn paentio darlun o'r Ddinas Sanctaidd, Gaersalem, mewn tristwch a diffeithwch: 'Mae hi'n wylo'n chwerw yn y nos; Ac mae ei dagrau ar ei bochau'. Mae, fodd bynnag, lygedyn o obaith; y gallem gael ein rhyddhau rhag poen drwy edrych ar y tristwch hwn, drwy dalu sylw (cenir 'attendite' yn Lladin bum gwaith yn y darn hwn, yn cynrychioli'r pum gwaith mae'n ymddangos yn Llyfr Galarnadau). Rwyf wedi dewis gosod y testun yn Lladin ac yn Saesneg ill dau gan ychwanegu llinell o Salm 133 yn Hebraeg tua'r diwedd: 'Wele mor dda, ac mor hyfryd yw, i frodyr drigo gyda'i gilydd mewn undod.'

## Ave Maria
(2008)

Ave Maria, gratia plena, Dominus tecum.
Benedicta tu in mulieribus,
et benedictus fructus ventris tui, Iesus.
Sancta Maria, Mater Dei,
ora pro nobis peccatoribus,
nunc et in hora mortis nostrae. Amen.

*Hail Mary, full of grace, the Lord is with thee.*
*Blessed art thou among women,*
*and blessed is the fruit of thy womb, Jesus.*
*Holy Mary, Mother of God,*
*pray for us sinners,*
*now and in the hour of our death. Amen.*

When I was a young boy I got lost in a graveyard near our home and, feeling alone and scared, took refuge in the small chapel there. Inside was a statue of the Blessed Virgin Mary with her arms outstretched, welcoming me. I felt saved, at peace, and just waited there until, shortly afterwards, I was found.
As I was writing this simple setting of one of the Christian Church's most powerful prayers, I was reminded of that time many years ago and something of those feelings of comfort and peace in the sight of our Blessed Lady found their way into this piece.

Pan oeddwn yn fachgen ifanc euthum ar goll mewn mynwent ger ein cartref ac yn teimlo'n unig ac yn ofnus, cefais loches yn y capel bach yno. Y tu mewn iddo oedd delwedd o'r Fendigaid Forwyn Fair â'i breichiau wedi'u hestyn allan, yn fy nghroesawu. Teimlais fel fy mod wedi fy achub, mewn heddwch, ac arhosais yno nes imi gael fy narganfod yn fuan wedyn. Wrth imi ysgrifennu'r trefniant syml hwn o un o weddïau mwyaf nerthol yr Eglwys Gristnogol, cefais fy atgoffa o'r adeg honno flynyddoedd maith yn ôl a daeth rhywbeth o'r teimladau hynny o gysur a heddwch yng ngolwg ein Bendigaid Forwyn i mewn i'r darn hwn.

## Locus Iste
(2009)

Locus iste a Deo factus est,
inaestimabile sacramentum;
irreprehensibilis est.

*This place was made by God,*
*a priceless sacrament;*
*beyond reproach.*

O flawless hallow, o seamless robe.
Lantern of stone, unbroken
*Peter Davidson*

This piece was commissioned by the University of Aberdeen for the quincentenary celebrations of King's College Chapel and is the third movement of my large cycle, 'Sanctuary Haunts'.
The text is from the Roman Catholic Mass for the Dedication of a Church with the addition of a few lines by the wonderful Scottish poet Peter Davidson: 'O Flawless hallow, O seamless robe, Lantern of stone unbroken'.

Comisiynwyd y darn hwn gan Brifysgol Aberdeen ar gyfer dathliadau pum can mlynedd Capel Coleg y Brenin a thrydydd symudiad fy nghylch mawr, 'Cynefinoedd Lloches' ydyw. Mae'r testun yn dod o'r Offeren Gatholig ar gyfer Cysegru Eglwys ag ychydig o linellau ychwanegol gan y bardd rhyfeddol o'r Alban, Peter Davidson: 'O gysegr Heb Fai, O wisg ddiwnïad, Lusern o gerrig di-dor'.

# Ubi caritas
(2011)

Ubi caritas et amor, Deus ibi est.
Congregavit nos in unum Christi amor.
Exultemus, et in ipso jucundemur.
Timeamus, et amemus Deum vivum.
Et ex corde diligamus nos sincero.
Amen

*Where charity and love are, God is there.*
*Christ's love has gathered us into one.*
*Let us rejoice and be pleased in Him.*
*Let us fear, and let us love the living God.*
*And may we love each other with a sincere heart.*
*Amen.*

Having heard a recording of *Now sleeps the crimson petal,* HRH Prince William of Wales and Catherine Middleton (now TRH The Duke and Duchess of Cambridge) chose it for their wedding in April 2011; however, after some debate, it was felt that the Tennyson words weren't appropriate for a religious service, so I suggested resetting them to the sixth-century Christian prayer, 'Ubi caritas' and this piece was born. I changed the word-setting, raised the key and included a fragment of the original plainsong at the end.

Wedi clywed recordiad o *Nawr cwsg y petal rhuddgoch,* dewisodd EUB y Tywysog William o Gymru a Catherine Middleton (erbyn hyn EHB Y Dug a'r Dduges o Gaergrawnt) hon ar gyfer eu priodas yn Ebrill 2011; fodd bynnag, ar ôl rhywfaint o drafod, teimlwyd nad oedd geiriau Tennyson yn briodol ar gyfer gwasanaeth crefyddol, felly awgrymais ei hailosod i'r weddi o'r chweched ganrif, 'Ubi caritas'. Newidiais drefniant y geiriau, codais y cywair a chynhwysais ran o'r blaengan wreiddiol ar y diwedd.

Your Guarantee of Quality:

As publishers, we strive to produce every book
to the highest commercial standards.

The music has been freshly engraved and the book
has been carefully designed to minimise awkward page turns
and to make playing from it a real pleasure.

Particular care has been given to specifying acid-free, neutral-sized paper made
from pulps which have not been elemental chlorine bleached.

This pulp is from farmed sustainable forests and
was produced with special regard for the environment.

Throughout, the printing and binding have been planned to ensure a sturdy,
attractive publication which should give years of enjoyment.

If your copy fails to meet our high standards,
please inform us and we will gladly replace it.

www.musicsales.com

Duration: 12 mins (approx)

# Now Sleeps The Crimson Petal

*Four Madrigals on Rose Texts for SATB (with divisi)*

PAUL MEALOR

*Commissioned by John Armitage Memorial*
*and first performed by the joint choirs of the University of St Andrews Chapel Choir,*
*University of Aberdeen Chamber Choir and the Edinburgh University Chamber Choir*
*Conducted by Michael Bawtree*
*October 28th, 29th & 31st 2010*

## *No. I: Now sleeps the crimson petal (Tennyson)*

*To Edward & Sarah Armitage with admiration and thanks*

*This may be sung by second sopranos only, or, the altos may be divided here instead

* Bracketed notes are optional divisi.

26
rit.
mf
o - pen un - to me. Now
o - pen un - to me. Now
o - pen un - to me.
o - pen un - to me.
B
30
poco rit.
mf
f
folds the li - ly all her sweet - ness up, And slips in - to the bo-som
folds the li - ly all her sweet - ness up, And slips in - to the bo-som
Now folds the li - ly all her sweet-ness up, And slips in - to the bo-som
Now folds the li - ly all her sweet-ness up, And slips in - to the bo-som

poco rit.
36
mf
of the lake: So fold thy - self, my dear - est,
of the lake: So fold thy - self, my dear - est,
of the lake: So fold thy - self, my dear - est,
of the lake: So fold thy - self, my dear - est,
poco rit.
40
ff
ppp
thou, and slip In - to my bo - som and be lost
thou, and slip In - to my bo - som and be lost
thou, and slip In - to my bo - som and be lost
thou, and slip In - to my bo - som and be lost
3
*This may be sung by second sopranos only, or, the Altos may be divided here instead

rall.
𝅗𝅥 = c. 48
mancando
45
in
me
unis.
ppp
Now
C
49
sleeps the crim-son pe - tal
now the white.

*To Eric von Ibler*
*& all my friends in the Edinburgh University Chamber Choir*

## *No. II: Lady, when I behold the roses sprouting (Anonymous)*

7
p
then be - hold your lips where sweet love har - bours, My
then be - hold your lips where sweet love har - bours,
then be - hold your lips where sweet love har - bours,
then be - hold your lips where sweet love har - bours,
10
mf
poco rit.
eyes pre - sent me with a dou - ble doubt - ing; For,
eyes pre - sent me with a dou - ble doubt - ing;
eyes pre - sent me with a dou - ble doubt - ing;
eyes pre - sent me with a dou - ble doubt - ing;

**A**

13

*f*

view - ing both a - like, view - ing both a - like, hard - ly my mind sup -

*f*

view - ing both a - like, view - ing both a - like, hard - ly my mind sup -

*f*

view - ing both a - like, view - ing both a - like, hard - ly my mind sup -

*f*

view - ing both a - like, view - ing both a - like, hard - ly my mind sup -

* Bracketed notes are optional divisi.

16

*pp* **molto rit.**

-po - ses Whe - ther the ro - ses be your lips or your lips the ro - ses.

*ppp*

-po - ses Ah, ro - ses.

*ppp*

-po - ses Ah, ro - ses.

*ppp*

-po - ses Ah, ro - ses.

*This may be sung by second sopranos only, if firsts cannot sing the low G♯; or, the Altos may be divided here instead

B
1st SOPRANOS
21
p
mf
Sopranos div.
Ah, ah,
2nd SOPRANOS & ALTOS
pp
p
La - dy, when I be - hold the ro - ses sprout - ing,
La - dy, when I be - hold the ro - ses sprout - ing, the ros - es,
La - dy, when I be - hold the ro - ses sprout - ing,
24
ah, ah,
ar - bours, and
Which clad in da - mask man - tles deck the ar - bours,
Which clad in da - mask man - tles deck the ar - bours, the ros - es,
Which clad in da - mask man - tles deck the ar - bours,

27
mf
ah,
ah,
ah,
then be - hold your lips where sweet love har - bours, My
then be - hold your lips where sweet love har - bours,
then be - hold your lips where sweet love har - bours,
30
f
poco rit.
ah,
ah,
ah.
For,
eyes pre - sent me with a dou - ble doubt - ing;
eyes pre - sent me with a dou - ble doubt - ing;
eyes pre - sent me with a dou - ble doubt - ing;

C
ALL SOPRANOS
33
ff
rit.
view - ing both a - like,
view - ing both a - like, hard -
ALL ALTOS
ff
view - ing both a - like,
view - ing both a - like, hard -
ff
view - ing both a - like,
view - ing both a - like, hard -
ff
view - ing both a - like,
view - ing both a - like, hard -
35
𝅗𝅥 = 62
-ly my mind sup - po - ses
ppp
-ly my mind sup - po - ses Whe -
-ly my mind sup - po - ses
-ly my mind sup - po - ses

37
Molto Rit.
ppp
Ah, ah, ah, ah,
-ther the ro - ses be your lips or your lips the ro - ses.
ppp
Ah, ro - ses.
ppp
Ah, ro - ses.
D
41
ppp
ah, ah, ah.
attacca
attacca
attacca
attacca

To Tom Wilkinson
& all my friends in the University of St Andrews Chapel Choir

# No. III: Upon a bank with roses set about (John Ward)

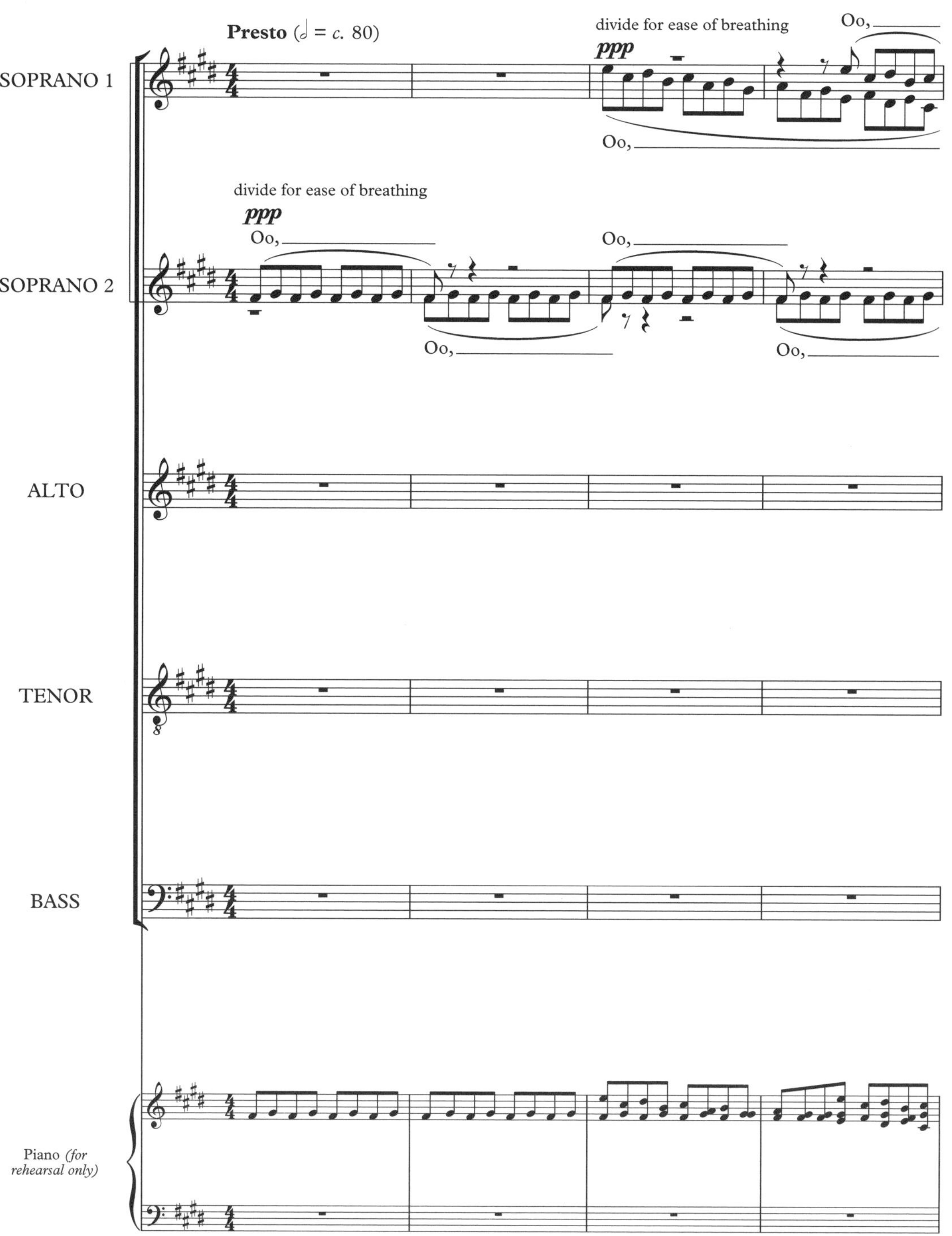

5
mf
Oo,
Oo,
ppp
Oo,
ppp
Oo,
A
8
Oo,
p
Oo,
p
divide for ease of breathing
Oo,
p
Oo,

B
12
pppp like an echo
Oo,
Oo,
p
Oo,
Oo,
Oo,
Oo,
Oo,
Oo,
Oo,
mf
Up - on a bank, up - on a bank with ro - ses set a - bout

15
Oo, Oo, Oo,
Oo, Oo, Oo,
Oo, Oo, Oo,
Oo, Oo, Oo,
Where pret-ty tur-tles join-ing bill to bill, and gen-tle springs steal soft-ly mur-mur-ing out,

C
18
(3+2+2)
p
Oo,
Oo,
pp
Wash-ing the foot of plea - sures sa - cred hill. There lit - tle love sore
Wash-ing the foot of plea - sures sa - cred hill. There lit - tle love sore
Wash-ing the foot of plea - sures sa - cred hill. There lit - tle love sore
Wash-ing the foot of plea - sures sa - cred hill. There lit - tle love sore
21
slow gliss.
wound - ed lies. His bow and ar - rows bro - ken,
wound - ed lies. His bow and ar - rows bro - ken,
wound - ed lies. His bow and ar - rows bro - ken,
wound - ed lies. His bow and ar - rows bro - ken,

25
Be - dewed with tears from Ve - nus' eyes.
Be - dewed with tears from Ve - nus' eyes.
Be - dewed with tears from Ve - nus' eyes.
Be - dewed with tears from Ve - nus' eyes.
28
rit.
p
Oo,
ppp
whispered
O gre - vious to be spo - ken
O gre - vious to be spo - ken
O gre - vious to be spo - ken
O gre - vious to be spo - ken

D
31
pp
pp
pp
Oo,
Oo,
Oo,
Oo,
Oo,
Oo,
Oo,
Oo,
Oo,
Oo,
Oo,
Oo,
Oo,
Oo,
Oo,
Oo,
3
8

35
mf
divisi
Oo,
Oo,
Up - on a bank, up - on a bank with ro - ses set a - bout Where pret - ty tur - tles
Oo,
Oo,
Oo,
Oo,
Oo,
Oo,
Oo,
Oo,
Oo,
mf
Up - on a bank, up - on a bank with ro - ses set a - bout Where pret - ty tur - tles join - ing

39
Oo,
Oo,
join - ing bill to bill, and gen - tle springs steal soft - ly mur - mur - ing
Oo,
Oo,
Oo,
Oo,
Oo,
Oo,
bill to bill, and gen - tle springs steal soft - ly mur - mur - ing out,

E
41
(3+2+2)
p
pp
Oo,
Wash - ing the foot of plea - sures sa - cred hill.
Wash - ing the foot of plea - sures sa - cred hill.
Wash - ing the foot of plea - sures sa - cred hill.
Wash - ing the foot of plea - sures sa - cred hill.
43
Oo,
slow gliss.
There lit - tle love sore woun - ded lies.
There lit - tle love sore woun - ded lies.
There lit - tle love sore woun - ded lies.
There lit - tle love sore woun - ded lies.

46
pp
Oo,
pp
Oo,
Oo,
pp
Oo,
Oo,
Oo,
F
49
Oo,
ppp
divide
Oo,
Oo,
ppp
divide
Oo,
Oo,
ppp
Oo,
Oo,

53
ppp
Oo,
Oo,
Oo,
Oo,
Oo,
56
pppp
ppppp
Oo,
Oo.

*To the memory of a wonderful lady, Audrey Halliwell*
*& to all my friends in the University of Aberdeen Chamber Choir*

# No. IV: A Spotless Rose (Anonymous)

* Bracketed notes are optional divisi.

B
Poco agitato
molto rit.
Is from its sweet root In Ma - ry,
Where - of I - si - ah said, spring - ing
sing - ing, ah, spring - ing
sing - ing, ah, spring - ing
Molto espressivo (𝅗𝅥 = c. 56)
poco rit.
pu - rest Maid; Ma-ry, pu - rest Maid; Ma-ry
ah, Through God's ah, The Bles - sed Babe
ah, Through God's great love and might ah, The Bles-sed Babe she bare us
ah, ah,

rit.
Molto espressivo (𝅗𝅥 = c. 50)
20
pp subito
pu - rest Maid; Through God's great love and
ah, Through God Through God's love and
f
ah, Through God's great love Through God's love and
ah, Through God's love and
C
Adagio, molto espressivo (𝅗𝅥 = c. 62)
22
ppp
might The Bless - ed Babe she bare us A - mid the cold, cold win - ter,

rit.
27
ppp
pp
and the dark mid - night.
The Bless - sed Babe she
D
30
Poco agitato
molto rit.
mf
p
Is from its sweet root In Ma - ry,
Through God's great love and might spring - ing
bare us
bare us ah, spring - ing
bare us ah, spring - ing

**Molto espressivo** (𝅗𝅥 = *c.* 56) **poco rit.** **poco rit.**

33

*f*

pu - rest Maid; Ma - ry, pu - rest Maid; Ma - ry,

ah, Through God's ah, The Bles - sed Babe

ah, Through God's great love and might ah, The Bles - sed Babe she bare us

Ah Ah

**rit.** **Molto espressivo** (𝅗𝅥 = *c.* 50)

35

*pp subito* *ppp*

pu - rest Maid; Through God's great love and might. A

ah, Through God Through God's love and might. A

ah, Through God's great love Through God's love and might. A

Ah Through God's love and might. A

E
38
p
Spot - less Rose is grow - ing,
Spot - less Rose is grow - ing, In a cold, cold win - ter's
Spot - less Rose is grow - ing, In a cold, cold win - ter's
Spot - less Rose is grow - ing, In a cold, cold win - ter's
41
ppp
F
Now sleeps the crim - son pe - tal.
night.
A - men.
night.
A - men.
night.
A - men.

Duration: 4 minutes (approx.)

*for Octavoce*

# She walks in beauty

*A setting of Lord Byron for SATB in 8 Parts*

PAUL MEALOR

A
poco rit.
rit.
11
to that ten-der light. Thus mel-lowed to that ten-der light. Thus mel-lowed to that ten-der
to that ten-der light. to that ten-der light. to that ten-der
to that ten-der light. to that ten-der light. to that ten-der
to that ten-der light. to that ten-der light. to that ten-der
16
(𝅗𝅥 = 64)
light. Which heav'n to gau - dy day de - nies
light. Which heav'n to gau - dy day de - nies
light. Which heav'n to gau - dy day de - nies
light. Which heav'n to gau - dy day de - de - nies

*Second Alto part hold note - gradually changing the shape of the vowel sound to 'Ah' - first Alto rest.
Second Alto part may divide for breathing purposes if more than one singer; however, if only one singer, breaths may be taken.

C
30
pp
Or soft - ly light - ens o'er her face;
pp
light - ens face;
ah,
pp
light - ens face;
34
unis.
poco rit.
Where thoughts se - rene - ly sweet ex - press how pure, how dear their dwell - ing place.
se - rene - ly sweet ex - press how pure, how dear their dwell - ing place.
unis.
'rene - ly sweet ex - press how pure, how dear their dwell - ing place.
pp
Ah
dear their dwell - ing place.

**D**

**poco rit.** **poco rit.**

39

*pp*

And on that cheek, and o'er that brow

*pp* *pp*

brow calm, yet el - o - quent

*pp* *pp*

Ah. So soft, so calm, yet el - o - quent

*pp* *pp*

Ah. calm, yet el - o - quent

* Bracketed notes are optional divisi.

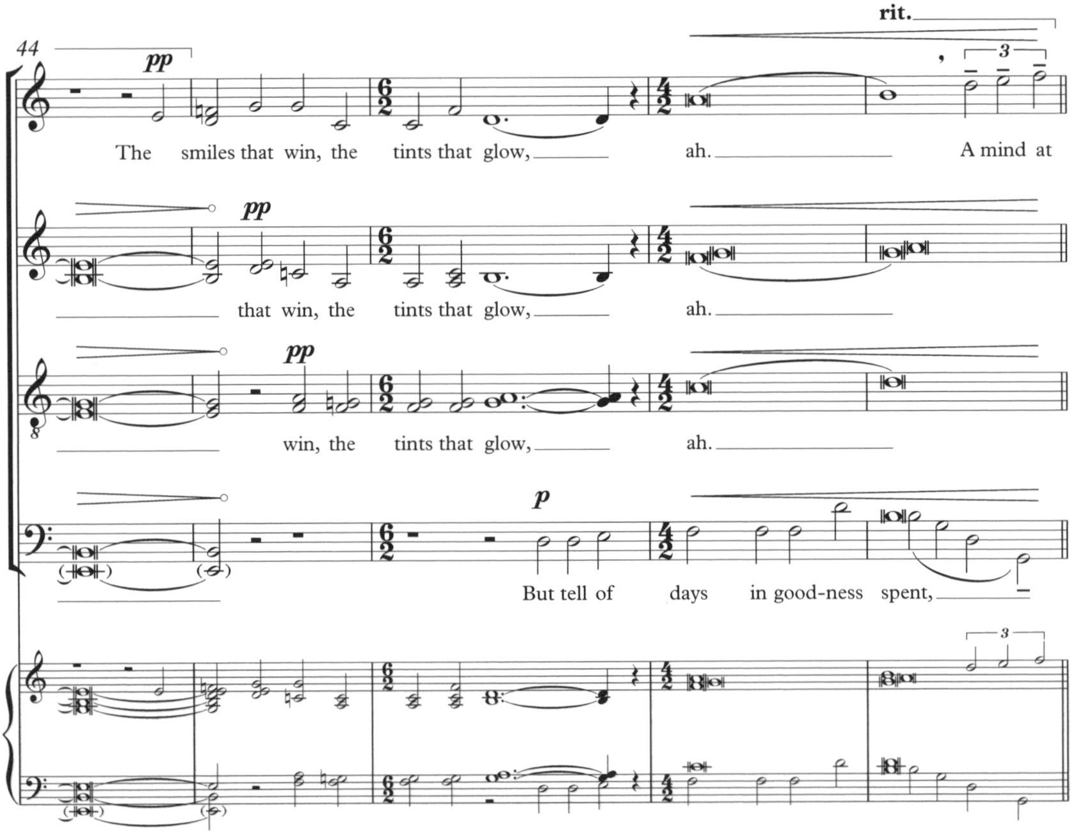

**rit.**

44

*pp*

The smiles that win, the tints that glow, ah. A mind at

*pp*

that win, the tints that glow, ah.

*pp*

win, the tints that glow, ah.

*p*

But tell of days in good-ness spent,

E
poco rit.
rit.
(𝅗𝅥 = 62)
peace with all be - low, a mind at peace with all be - low, a mind at peace with all be -
peace with all be - low, peace with all be - low, peace with all be -
- low, a heart whose love is in - no - cent.
- low, a heart whose love is in - no - in - no - cent.

**F**

59

***pppp*** *like a whisper...*

One shade the more, one ray the less,

***pppp*** *like a whisper...*

more, less,

* Ah.

***pppp*** *like a whisper...*

more, less,

**molto rit.**

63

unis.

whose love is in - no - cent.

in - no - cent, in - no - cent.

***pppp***

in - no - cent.

***pppp***

in - no - cent.

*Second Alto part hold note – gradually changing the shape of the vowel sound to 'Ah' – first Alto rest.
Second Alto part may divide for breathing purposes if more than one singer; however, if only one singer, breaths may be taken.

Duration: 4 minutes (approx.)

*For Ralph Allwood*

# O vos omnes

*for SATB (with divisi) & Tubular Bells*

PAUL MEALOR

*O all you who walk by on the road, pay attention and see:*
*if there is any sorrow like my sorrow.*
*Pay attention, all people, and look at my sorrow.*
Lamentations 1:12

*Behold how good, and how pleasant it is,*
*For brothers to dwell together in unity.*
Psalm 133, vs. 1

5
rall.
mf
f
-si - tis per vi - am,
mf
f
-si - tis per vi - am,
mf
f
-si - tis per vi - am,
mf
f
-si - tis per vi - am,
Bracketed notes may be omitted
if thought too low for the section.
A
8
rall.
ff l.v.
pp l.v.
ff
at - ten - di - te
Si
ff
p
at - ten - di - te
vi - de - te:
Si
Bracketed notes may be omitted if thought
too high, or uncomfortable, for the section.
ff
p
at - ten - di - te et vi - de - te:
p
vi - de - te:

13
B
1.
l.v.
pp
est do - lor si - mi - lis si - cut do - lor me - us. Si
est do - lor si - mi - lis si - cut do - lor me - us. Si
2.
rall.
17
mf
l.v. sempre
ff
Si
cut do - lor me - us. Si est do - lor
cut do - lor me - us. Si est do - lor
p
Si est do - lor
Si est do - lor

23
C
fff
l.v.
fff
At - ten - di - te, at -
fff
At - ten - di - te, at -
fff
At - ten - di - te, at -
fff
ah
25
rall.
-ten - di - te, at - ten - di -
-ten - di - te, at - ten - di -
-ten - di - te, at - ten - di -
ah
ah

D
28
ffff
l.v.
- te,
at -
- te,
at -
- te,
at -
ah
29
rall.
fff
f
l.v.
ppp l.v.
- ten - di - te.
- ten - di - te.
- ten - di - te.
ah
ah

E
34
rall.
pp
l.v.
pp<
pp<
vos om - nes,
vos om - nes
ppp
O vos om - nes,
O vos om - nes
ppp
O vos om - nes,
O vos om - nes
ppp
O vos om - nes,
O vos om - ne(s)
(gradually change 'vowel' sound)
F
Adagissimo, molto rubato (𝅗𝅥 = c. 48)
40
lunga
Solo - a piacere.
molto rubato
p
Pay at-ten-tion, all peo - ple, and look at my
pppp
(Breath when needed)
ah

43
...an echo...
l.v.
...an echo...
l.v.
sor - row. My
sor - row. My
47
Solo – a piacere.
molto rubato – distant
pppp
ppp l.v.
Hi-nei ma tov u-ma na im, she-vet a-chim gam ya - chad.
sor - row.

Duration: 6 mins (approx.)

*for Sir Duncan Rice*

# Locus Iste

*Commissioned by the University of Aberdeen*
*to celebrate the 500th anniversary of the consecration of King's College Chapel*
*and premiered by Polyphony, conducted by Stephen Layton.*

PAUL MEALOR

*This place was made by God,*
*a priceless sacrament;*
*beyond reproof.*

*O Flawless hallow, O seamless robe.*
*Lantern of stone, unbroken.*
*(Peter Davidson)*

A
7
rit.
(no breath)
pp
mf
lo - cus i - ste, lo - cus i - ste lo - cus i - ste
(no breath)
pp
mf
lo - cus i - ste, lo - cus i - ste lo - cus i - ste
(no breath)
pp
mf
lo - cus i - ste, lo - cus i - ste lo - cus i - ste
pp
mf
lo - cus i - ste, lo - cus i - ste lo - cus i - ste
molto rit.
[♩ = 64]
molto rit.
13
f
ff
lo - cus i - ste a De - o fac - tus est,
f
ff
lo - cus i - ste a De - o fac - tus est,
f
ff
lo - cus i - ste a De - o fac - tus est, in ae - sti -
(Tenor 2: no breath)
f
ff
lo - cus i - ste a De - o fac - tus est,

**B**

17 **a tempo (♩ = 68)**

*pp* *mf*

in - ae - sti - ma - bi - le,

*pp* *mf*

in - ae - sti - ma - bi - le ah, in - ae - sti - ma - bi - le,

*pp* *mf*

- ma - bi - le ah, ah, sa - cra -

*pp* *mf*

ma - bi - le ah, ah,

22 **molto rit.**

*f* *ff*

sa - cra - men - tum, sa - cra - men - tum,

*f* *ff*

in - ae - sti - ma - bi - le, in - ae - sti - ma - bi - le ah,

*f* *ff*

- men - tum, ah, ah,

Solo

*f* *ff*

ah, ah, sa - cra -

[♩ = 62]
molto rit.
27
pp
ppp
ah,
sa - cra - men - tum,
Solo
p
tutti
sa - cra - men - tum,
Sa - cra - men - tum,
- men - tum; ir - re - pre - hen - si - bi - lis est
C
a tempo (♩ = 68)
rit.
33
mf
Lo - cus i - ste, lo - cus i - ste a De - o fac - tus est,

39
rit.
pp
(no breath)
lo - cus i - ste, lo - cus i - ste
pp
(no breath)
lo - cus i - ste, lo - cus i - ste
pp
(no breath)
lo - cus i - ste, lo - cus i - ste
pp
lo - cus i - ste, lo - cus i - ste
43
rit.
mf
f
lo - cus i - ste lo - cus i - ste in -
mf
f
lo - cus i - ste lo - cus i - ste in -
mf
f
lo - cus i - ste lo - cus i - ste in -
mf
f
lo - cus i - ste lo - cus i - ste in -

D
♩ = c. 64
47
rit.
rit.
ff
-ae - sti - ma - bi - le, in - ae - sti - ma - bi - le in - ae - sti - ma - bi -
in - ae - sti - ma - bi - le in - ae - sti - ma - bi -
-ae - sti - ma - bi - le, sa - cra men - tum sa - cra - men - tum
-ae - sti - ma - bi - le, in - ae - sti - ma - bi - le, in - ae - sti - ma - bi -
-ae - sti - ma - bi - le, in - ae - sti - ma - bi - le, in - ae - sti - ma - bi -
52
rit.
fff
mf
pp
-le, in - ae - sti - ma - bi - le, in - ae - sti - ma - bi - le
-le, in - ae - sti - ma - bi - le, sa - cra - men - tum
-le, in - ae - sti - ma - bi - le in - ae - sti - ma - bi - le
-le, in - ae - sti - ma - bi - le, in - ae - sti - ma - bi - le

E
♩ = c. 60
rit.
rit.
57
ppp
mf
Lo - cus i - ste, lo - cus i - ste a De - o fac - tus est,
Lo - cus i - ste, lo - cus i - ste a De - o fac - tus est,
Lo - cus i - ste, lo - cus i - ste a De - o fac - tus est,
Lo - cus i - ste, lo - cus i - ste a De - o fac - tus est,
F
♩ = c. 56
like a whisper
63
pppp
Lo - cus i - ste, lo - cus i - ste
Lo - cus i - ste, lo - cus i - ste
Lo - cus i - ste, lo - cus i - ste
Lo - cus i - ste, lo - cus i - ste

*Soloist should hold the pause until choir has completed its cycle of repeats.
At Section G, soloist and choir should now sing at the same tempo, approx. ♩ = 52.
Molto Rubato (♩ = c. 52)
SOPRANO SOLO (independent of choir)
67
p
mf
O flaw-less hal-low, o seam-less robe. Lan-tern of stone, un-bro-ken
Molto Rubato (♩ = c. 56)
Lo - cus i - ste.
Lo - cus i - ste.
Lo - cus i - ste.
Lo - cus i - ste.
**SATB should repeat 'boxed' section, including pauses and breaks for breathing at the steady tempo of ♩ = 56, independent of soprano soloist.

G
74
♩ = c. 52
rit.
O flaw - less hal - low
♩ = c. 52
rit.
Bell-like ppp
San - tu - a - ri - o
A - - - - - men.
A - - - - - men.
A - - - - - men.

Duration: 7 mins (approx.)

# Ave Maria

PAUL MEALOR

*Hail Mary, full of grace, the Lord is with thee;*
*blessed art thou among women,*
*and blessed is the fruit of thy womb, Jesus.*

*Holy Mary, Mother of God,*
*pray for us sinners,*
*now and at the hour of our death.*

*Amen*

A
5
pp
rit.
pp
gra - ti - a ple - na, Do - mi - nus te - cum; Be - ne - dic - ta tu in
pp
pp
gra - ti - a ple - na, Do - mi - nus te - cum; Be - ne - dic - ta tu in
pp
pp
gra - ti - a ple - na, Do - mi - nus te - cum; dic - ta tu in
pp
pp
ple - na, Do - mi - nus te - cum; in
10
rit.
mf
mu - li - er - i - bus, et be - ne - dic - tus fruc - tus
mf
mu - li - er - i - bus, et be - ne - dic - tus fruc - tus
mf
mu - li - er - i - bus, et be - ne - dic - tus fruc - tus
mf
fruc - tus
mu - li - er - i - bus, be - ne - dic - tus fruc - tus

rit.
rit.
14
f
ppp
ven - tris tu - i, Je - sus. A - ve Ma - ri - a.
ven - tris tu - i, Je - sus. A - ve ri - a.
ven - tris tu - i, Je - sus. A - ve ri - a. Sanc - ta Ma -
ven - tris tu - i, Je - sus. A - ve ri - a.
* Bracketed notes are optional divisi.
B
19
p
mf
f
Sanc - ta Ma - ri - a, Ma - ter De - i
Sanc - ta Ma - ri - a, Ah,
- ri - a, Ma - ri - a Ah,
Ma - ri - a, Ah,

24
rit.
mf
p
or - a pro no - bis pec-ca-tor - i - bus,
Sanc - ta Ma -
Ah,
Ah.
Sanc - ta Ma - ri - a,
Sanc - ta Ma - ri - a,
Ma - ri - a
29
pp
-ri - a, Sanc-ta Ma - ri - a, Sanc-ta Ma - ri - a,
Ah, Ah, Ah.
Ma - ri - a Ah, Ah, Ah. nunc et in

35
rit.
ho - ra mor - tis no - strae.
ho - ra mor - tis no - strae.
C
40
ppp
A - ve, A - ve, A - ve Ma - ri - a,
A - ve, A - ve, A - ve Ma - ri - a,
A - ve, A - ve, A - ve Ma - ri - a,
A - ve, A - ve, A - ve Ma - ri - a,

D
45
p
mf
rit.
f
gra - ti - a ple - na, Dom - i - nus te cum; Be - ne - dic - tus tu - in
gra - ti - a ple - na, Dom - i - nus te cum; Be - ne - dic - tus tu - in
gra - ti - a ple - na, Dom - i - nus te cum; dic - tus tu - in
ple - na, Dom - i - nus te cum; in
50
rit.
ff
mu - li - e - ri - bus, et be - ne - dic - tus fruc - tus ven - tris
mu - li - e - ri - bus, et be - ne - dic - tus fruc - tus ven - tris
mu - li - e - ri - bus, et be - ne - dic - tus fruc - tus ven - tris
mu - li - e - ri - bus, be - ne - dic - tus fruc - tus ven - tris

54
fff
rit.
tu - i, Je - sus. A - ve Ma - ri -
tu - i, Je - sus. A - ve Ma - ri -
tu - i, Je - sus. A - ve Ma - ri -
tu - i, Je - sus. A - ve Ma - ri -
58
-a, et be - ne - dic - tus fruc - tus ven - tris tu - i,
tu - i,
-a, et be - ne - dic - tus fruc - tus ven - tris tu
-a, et be - ne - dic - tus fruc - tus ven - tris tu - i,
1st Bass only
fruc - tus tu
-a, et be - ne - dic - tus fruc - tus ven - tris tu - i,

molto rit.
62
Je - sus. A - ve Ma - ri - a
Je - sus. A - ve Ma - ri - a
Je - sus. A - ve Ma - ri - a
Je - sus. A - ve Ma - ri - a
E
66
ppp
A - ve, A - ve, A - ve Ma - ri - a
A - ve, A - ve, A - ve Ma - ri - a
A - ve, A - ve, A - ve Ma - ri - a
A - ve, A - ve, A - ve Ma - ri - a

mancando
70
p
A - ve, Ma - ri - a,
p
Ah, Ma - ri - a,
pp
TENOR SOLO
Sanc - ta Ma -
p
Ah, Ma - ri - a,
p
Ah, Ma - ri - a,
74
pppp
Ma - ri - a.
pppp
pppp
Ma - ri A - men.
When singing the letter 'n',
close the lips to a 'hum' and
then dim. to silence...
- ri - a.
pppp
pppp
Ma - ri A - men.
pppp
pppp
Ma - ri A - men.

Duration: 4 mins (approx.)

*Dedicated to*
*Their Royal Highnesses The Duke & Duchess of Cambridge*
*with respectful good wishes*

# Ubi caritas

*for SATB (with divisi)*

*Composed for the Marriage of His Royal Highness Prince William of Wales, K.G. with Miss Catherine Middleton and first performed by the Choirs of Westminster Abbey and Her Majesty's Chapel Royal, St James's Palace, conducted by James O'Donnell, at Westminster Abbey, Friday, 29th April 2011.*

PAUL MEALOR

*Where charity and love are, God is there.*
*Christ's love has gathered us into one.*
*Let us rejoice and be pleased in Him.*
*Let us fear, and let us love the living God.*
*And may we love each other with a sincere heart.*

**Adagio, molto espressivo** (𝅗𝅥 = *c.* 48)

poco rit.

ppp pp p

SOPRANO: U - bi ca - ri - tas et a - mor, De - us

ALTO: U - bi ca - ri - tas et a - mor, De - us

TENOR: mor, De - us

BASS: mor, De - us

Piano (*for rehearsal only*)

poco rit.
6
mf
i - bi est. Con - gre -
i - bi est. Con - gre -
i - bi est. Con - gre -
i - bi est. Con - gre -
poco rit.
10
f
poco
- ga - vit nos in un - um Chri - sti a - mor.
- ga - vit nos in un - um Chri - sti a - mor.
- ga - vit nos in un - um Chri - sti a - mor.
- ga - vit nos in un - um Chri - sti a - mor.

A

14

poco rit.

ppp

Ex - ul - te-mus, et in ip - so ju-cun - de - mur. Ex - ul -

Ex - ul - te-mus, et in ip - so ju-cun - de - mur. Ex - ul -

Ex - ul - te-mus, et in ip - so ju-cun - de - mur. Ex - ul -

Ex - ul - te-mus, et in ip - so ju-cun - de - mur. Ex - ul -

19

ppp

-te - mus. Ti-me - a-mus, et a - me-mus De - um

-te - mus. Ti-me - a - mus, et a - me-mus De - um

-te - mus. Ti-me - a - mus, et a - me-mus De - um

-te - mus. Ti-me - a - mus, et a - me-mus De - um

molto rit.
24
vi - vum. Et ex cor - de di - li - ga - mus nos sin - ce - ro.
vi - vum. Et ex cor - de di - li - ga - mus nos sin - ce - ro.
vi - vum. Et ex cor - de di - li - ga - mus nos sin - ce - ro.
vi - vum. Et ex cor - de di - li - ga - mus nos sin - ce - ro.
* Bracketed notes are optional divisi.
B
poco rit.
30
mf
f
U - bi ca - ri - tas et a - mor, De - us i -
U - bi ca - ri - tas et a - mor, De - us i -
U - bi ca - ri - tas et a - mor, De - us i -
U - bi ca - ri - tas et a - mor, De - us i -

poco rit.
36
mf
ff
poco rit.
-bi est. Con-gre - ga-vit nos in un-um Chri-sti a - mor.
-bi est. Con-gre - ga-vit nos in un-um Chri-sti a - mor.
-bi est. Con-gre - ga-vit nos in un-um Chri-sti a - mor.
-bi est. Con-gre - ga-vit nos in un-um Chri-sti a - mor.
42
ppp
molto rit.
De - us i - bi est, i - bi est.
De - us i - bi est, i - bi est.
De - us i - bi est, i - bi est.
De - us i - bi est, i - bi est.

C
mancando 𝅗𝅥 = c. 44
Solo
(This may be sung 'off stage' if desired)
49
ppp
U - bi ca - ri - tas et a - mor.
U - bi ca - ri -
ppp
U - bi ca - ri - tas et a - mor.
ppp
A - men.
ppp
A - men.
55
-tas et a - mor
ppp
A - men.
ppp
A - men.
ppp
A - men.